Why Trees Sneeze
and Other Mysteries

Why Trees Sneeze
and Other Mysteries

Poems by

Curt G. Curtin

© 2021 Curt G. Curtin. All rights reserved.
This material may not be reproduced in any form, published,
reprinted, recorded, performed, broadcast,
rewritten or redistributed without
the explicit permission of Curt G. Curtin.
All such actions are strictly prohibited by law.

Cover design by Shay Culligan

Library of Congress number 2021946844

ISBN: 978-1-63980-025-4

Kelsay Books
502 South 1040 East, A-119
American Fork, Utah 84003
Kelsaybooks.com

Acknowledgments

Special thanks to photographers who made their beautiful photos available through Unsplash.com:

Front cover photo:

Children in Park Throwing Up Yellow Autumn Leaves
　　　by Vitolda Klein at (unsplash.com/photos/6bp-luTzBDE)

Back cover photo:

Blue Footed Booby by Hans Jurgen-Mager at
　　　(unsplash.com/photos/6hD_CcqROc)

Contents

Why Trees Sneeze	11
Why Rivers Shiver	12
Why Oaks Talk That Way	13
Garden Variety Verse	14
Fire Hydrants	16
Our TV	17
My Father's Truck	18
Yellow School Bus	19
Some Trees I've Known	20
Dances With Trees	21
Squat Geese	22
Sparrows	23
Rex That Pecks	24
Never Swallow Mints Whole	25
Chrystal Sings	26
in Just—	27
Zirafah, Tall and Slender	28
Blue-footed Boobies	29
Halloween	30
Apples and Oranges	32
Making Waves	33
An Inconsideration of Cats	34
Ms. Mockingbird	35
Teacher, help me, pleeze!	36
How a Lepidoptera Survived A Rapid Rapids Ride	37

Why Trees Sneeze

Ivy Vine is domineering. She makes
her leaves lick shins of trees
to make them shiver from bottom to top.
She knows it constricts the cricks in veins,
and that's the trick that makes trees sneeze;
and when trees sneeze they send their leaves
flying for miles in terrible pain,
and none of them ever gets home again.

Old Dan Moss, on the other hand,
caresses trees with the softest touch—
a little itch, but not too much—
and when their skin is hard and tight
his touch is light and nicely moist,
just the choice the tree would make
if it could say to the forest floor,
"I'll have some moss please, nothing more."

Why Rivers Shiver

You could say that rivers shiver 'cause
the rocks along the bottom wear no socks.
Stones can be bone chilling if you sit
on them in winter, but this is really silly.
I'm sure you know that rivers never sit.

You could say that rivers shiver 'cause
the fish are weighing currentcy on scales.
When they wiggle they deliver silver shivers.
But this is just ridiculous. You know that
rivers always keep their silver in the bank.

You could say that rivers shiver 'cause
a waterfall is calling them to play, and
they're scared when they dive that they won't
come up alive. That's absurd, and I'm sure
you've heard it said that they dive on a bed.

The reason rivers shiver is they're open to the sky
when the wind is passing by. As you know,
the wind has fingers that can tickle, and the
happy river giggles as it wriggles—you can
hear it if you try. That is why a river shivers.

Why Oaks Talk That Way

You know that oaks are big and strong,
bigger than a mastodon. You know
they must be very proud to speak aloud
up there among the puffed up clouds.
The trouble is that all day long
they choose to speak in platitudes,
address the world with boring views
and pompous, empty attitudes.

I do know where they learned that speech,
and you do too, you just forgot while you
were saying "frogs knit socks for dogs."

What chatters on the oaks all day,
skitters like a silly twit and thinks it's
witty while it gathers bitter acorns?
What chitters chatters blithers blathers,
(Go back and say that line again.)
What chitters chatters blithers blathers,
(Well, you almost got it then.)
and tattles tales that never matter?

An oak that lives a hundred years and hears
that kind of talk all day has just become
another guy who thinks it must be very wise
never to extemporize, but just repeat what
every day a billion blathering squirrels say.

Garden Variety Verse

I do reply to a proud banana,
if he keeps his skin on when he talks.
I often speak with veggies, too, as long as
they're not in a stew. It would be rude
to refuse. The peas, indeed, are most
polite, are pleased to be seen at all.
Even the string beans, though they're tart,
have mastered the art of greenish speech,
and underneath that quiet shell
they have the sense to speak quite well.

I'm especially fond of corn. They're
proud, you know. That's why they wear
their hair in a plume and keep their ears
well groomed.—At this, the proud banana
sniffed and said that corn, when stripped,
was never as fine as he. I didn't reply.
Besides, because he never exercised
I saw that he was getting soft.

I do not dare forget the cabbage, whose
heads are packed with crackley speech,
but talking heads so seldom listen;
they think you love to hear them preach.
I think that beets could teach them how
to speak of deeper matter. Beets, of course,
are so, well, red, that I must blush to say

I'm only half as bright as they. I've heard
it said they're so well read they argue with
the cauliflower (whose heads look so much
like a brain they must contain enough deep
thoughts to fill a chowder pot.) That's a lot!
If you don't mind, I think we're finished.
I'm going to whisper with some spinach.

Fire Hydrants

It's not that they have no sense of humor
(they're known to gush when tickled by flushing),
but they never seem to grin.
It isn't because they're ugly (which is true)
or almost never speak to you
(they're dull as a stump when they do); no,
they're taught to tightly hold their sides
to hold a city's water supplies
for fire and ice and fluffy rice
and making you smell nice.
So you could try to make them smile
by one of your amazing tricks.
You put both hands across their hats
I know that helps them to relax (unlike
what they endure from dogs or even cats.)
Then you hop across their tops
like fleas that leap across your knees.

Our TV

Our TV is on all day,
it's on all night
until the lights go out.
We've learned to think
and even wink
in sync with it.
It's time to eat
when we're repeating
ads for whiter teeth,
time to sleep
when all that sound
begins to drown my mind,
time to wake
        when my TV beside my
        head bores deep within
        my sleeping brain—
        it's so inane!
        Click.

My Father's Truck

My Dad's truck clatters like
falling stacks of iron racks.
The tailgate bangs like a jail cell door,
the hood is dented, bumper bent,
and he says where the hubcaps went is—
well, there may be one downstairs.
The left door closes with a crunch.
The other's red—the truck is blue,
I guess you'd say one door is new,
except the handle's broken too.
Signals sometimes light for turns,
but can you tell me what is worse
than signals working in reverse?
Mornings when I miss the bus
and simply must get in to school,
I cross my fingers, say a prayer,
and let my Dad's truck take me there.
Everybody hears us coming.
Students line the street to cheer.
High upon my rattling stage
I wave to all my loyal fans,
then descend in royal manner.
Envy glows on many faces
as my chauffer drives away,
each one wishing for a father
who could make such grand display.

Yellow School Bus

On the early streets sleepy children
with sacks and caps that advertise
bobble and bop through folding doors
to ride like eggs in a yellow bucket.

At each new stop they juggle their sacks
and talk to the new arrivals who
walk the aisle like frantic chickens
seeking a friend to hop beside.

After school the yellow buckets
are back to pack us up inside,
eggs with legs and noisy chickens
happy to bop and cackle and ride.

Some Trees I've Known

(Trees agree on difference; that's natural selection.
But each agree that being tree is natural perfection.)

Alder feed on gossip gleaned from small, impatient
streams. Sated, slow, they love the shallow flow.

With muscular weave of marbled arms and awesome height
beech make airy rooms that illumine uses of light.

Apple trees have crooked joints, hands that droop
when filled with fruit. Poor dears, I fear they are arthritic.

Pines, well you know pines; always on the move,
they wave goodbye. You know they never mean to go.

Oaks hold weights to make their muscles bold, they shape
their skin with ragged winds, and dry leaves hang in snow.

Redwoods bellow when they fall, roar down sky,
pull down the moon, mar the ground and howl of doom.

Hemlocks suck on rocks and snort ice.

Dances With Trees

Trees never wander. There's a reason,
but we'll let it go for now. For now,
it's quite enough to know that though
it's true no trees can walk, it's also true
they can can-can and can demand to dance.

Of course we'll need to re-define some terms,
like stride, slide, strut, caper, cavort,
gavotte and entrechat. Some do plie,
and so do we, so that will stay the way it is,
but with no feet the beat for trees is not so easy.

Most trees dance above the waist, most with
easy grace; but baobabs grow hip to crown, and
banyan's arms grow roots that hold them down.
There must be others that, like you and me,
can't dance like other versions of a tree.

We know that willows swing their hips
(we see the swaying of their gowns),
and burly oak dance dignified and slow.
Aspen move so cool, they gesture as they bend,
but they giggle when they're tickled by the wind.

When trees grow old they dance a graceful,
grave and elegant ballet, but only when they want to.
At other times they mambo, rock and bunny-hop,
shrug and jive and jitterbug, then go to sleep to keep
the color in their cheeks, but only when they want to.

Squat Geese

Squat geese feed like fat old crows.
They waddle heavy by the shore,
float like fat boots on the water.

They talk in sesquipedalian squawks
that mock each other's remarks, and
even I can't bear to hear them sing.

But then one day, with a heavy lift
they fly with grace that makes you sigh,
sleek as only geese can be
                against
                          the
                                  sky.

Sparrows

Sparrows walk in hops
as if on pogo sticks.
Seagulls waddle
side to side.
Why?

Sparrows fly by flitting
oh so zig-zag quick.
Seagulls float like kites
on high. Why?

And why can't I?

Rex That Pecks

From the fossil of a thunder lizard
DNA was plucked and analyzed.
To everyone's surprise that ugly hide
was found to be an ancient kin
of the cackle racket barnyard hen
and the wicked bruiser rooster.
Have you ever tried to make friends
with a hen? I'm sure you'll agree
as well with me, the rooster is
a frightful thing; it may be a bird,
but have you ever heard it sing?
The fluffy chicken may be cute
and please us with its little peeps,
but when it grows and has long claws,
pause before you pet its pretty neck.
This Tyrannosaurus pecks.

Never Swallow Mints Whole

Slowly slow think luscious mints
that slide on sweet juice pools you
hold and roll within your cheeks. We
say slow slowly just to let you know
the pleasure, to be whole, must be
slowly rolled; just to say that mints
sing only when they slowly slide
inside full pools held a honeyed
while on deeply sweetened tongues.

Chrystal Sings

Chrystal is two and has learned to sing.
Well, not just now. She sang in her crib
before she could even say, Ole!
Then she learned a song of shrieks,
each more wonderful than the last;
and even gasps had sharps and flats,
and meaning quite beyond my hearing.

So Chrystal sings to a world amazed;
well, me at least. You would know
much better than I what she reveals
because you sing whatever pleases you,
while I must check the critics, who
write essays to inform; and after all,
Chrystal is still in in-form-a-tion now.

in Just—

A seven-year-old can jump and run;
oh yes, I've seen them bounce repeatedly
at the thought of the thought of ice cream,
of a new toy, a holiday, being asked
to sing or play, or Just—a bit of silliness.
Oh yes, a seven-year-old can jump and run.

A seven-year-old can take a stand
to leave some heavy greens upon her plate,
to beg and beg to stay awake past eight,
to please insist that gramma stay the night,
can face the dark alone in spite of trolls
or stand alone against a bully's growls.

AND a seven-year-old can see an evil
that it never can elude or undo.

For the children in too many places.

Zirafah, Tall and Slender

Zirafah, tall and slender, walks with a gingerly pace,
alone and strange along the streets of old Savannah.
She knows she arrived in a crate that was roughly placed
on a long, grey dock by the river that ran to the sea.

Zirafah, tall and slender, peers around each corner long
before she turns, searching for signs of lions. Beneath
the leafless trees all hung with leafless vines, no sign
of lions, but other creatures call and come too near.

Zirafah hugs a stucco wall almost the color she knew
herself to be, and blends with it for safety; but when she
lifts her eyes a square of light appears, shining and clear.
There, at a height like hers, two large and frightened eyes.

The world has many surprises. Imagine Zirafah's eyes
in a window pane. Everything is wild until it is named.
If I tell you her name you may be surprised, but you
will realize that she is so very far from her savannah.

---

zirafah: an Arabic word
(giraffa: Italian, from the Arabic)

Blue-footed Boobies

Dozens of blue-footed boobies rise
without a word from a boss bird.
It's as if an invisible slippery hand
had slid beneath the booby clan
and lifted them all to swirl and whirl
above a rough Galapagos shore
where loggerhead turtles, one by one,
lie like logs on the rocks and snore.

The boobies fly, not one by one,
but in a galactic uniform storm,
into bright tides in regular motion
into the krill filled whale road known
as the great Pacific Ocean.
Blue-footed boobies don't ask why;
they fly and dive because—well,
why do you ask why? It's just the way
that they survive. If you were a blue-
footed booby that's the way you'd fly.

Blue-footed boobies live in the Galapagos Islands
in the Pacific Ocean.

Halloween

Who-oo-oo, Who-oo-oo
What's that coming down the hall?
Sounds like something eight feet tall,
head against the ceiling, arms against the wall,
and that isn't all.

Who-oo-oo, Who-oo-oo
What's that coming down the hall?
It has ten fingers and perhaps eleven toes,
twenty big teeth and a big blue nose,
there's more, you know.

Who-oo-oo, Who-oo-oo
What's that coming down the hall?
Its mouth is open and its breath is foul,
its lips are moving and it isn't just growl,
and it's drooling now.

Who-oo-oo, Who-oo-oo
What's that coming down the hall?
I think I hear a sniffle and a snuffle and a wheeze,
I think I hear a burp and a "Pardon me, please,"
then a huge sneeze.

Who-oo-oo, Who-oo-oo
What's that coming down the hall?
Oh, it wheezed by my door and it sneezed like a sow,
and it snuffled like a rabbit and gave its nose a blow.
What a show!

Who-oo-oo, Who-oo-oo
What's that coming down the hall?
Well, it looked at me with its bloodshot eyes,
then gave another sneeze and apologized.
Was I surprised!
(Guess who.)

Apples and Oranges

I'm an old man, my name is Sam.
My age is two times thirty,
minus five, and add fifteen,
and when you're done
then add some ones.
Divide by sad and happy days
and write that down with no delay.
That's not the sum,
there's more to come.

I'm six feet tall, my eyes are brown,
I do wear shoes when I'm in town,
I sing the blues when feeling good
and when my mood is very low
I laugh a lot more than I should.
Since you've heard the evidence
and think it makes a lot of sense,
it's time for you to make a guess,
impress me with your estimate.
How old was I when you were born?
Now isn't this an easy test?

—Put estimate here: (   )

Making Waves

I could say that it's all about gravity,
attraction the motions of planets make
as they ride like bowls in a wide whirlpool;
but if you ask me, I think the waves
are made by singers who live in caves
under the sea. Their singing moves
the sea anemone to undulate in wet gyrations,
as you'd expect them to. You know, they imitate.
In each long line the wave waifs hold
each other's hands and leap to reach the grass
that waves atop the wind-blown dune
in imitation of sea anemones.
As for the moon—that some say makes
the tides—it always responds to the songs
of grav-i-tational singers under the sea.

An Inconsideration of Cats

(with a catch-all cat call to T.S. Eliot)

Twenty-four tiger cats rolled in a ball
went hissing and spitting down through a Mall.
They raged like a furnace and roared like a gale,
having spent all their cash at a catnip sale.

Imagine a caucus of calico cats
debating the matter of mice versus rats
while every persuasion and arty of bats
strolled under their noses and over their spats.

Two lady angoras in elegant furs
were heard ostentatiously speaking in purrs;
"The attention of Toms is a tedious curse."
"Yes, dahling, but not the assent it infers."

Ninety-six red cats one night late
passed by black cats, eight-by-eight.
If you were there you'd speculate,
"That's a red-hot fire in a coal-black grate."

The rudest of the cats is the Manx.
They're short with their answers, cantankerous cranks.
Though you speak without limit admiring their flanks,
if you tell them a tale they will never say thanks.

T.S. Elliot was a famous poet who wrote many poems included in a book for children titled: *Old Possum's Book of Practical Cats*. The musical "Cats" used many of these poems in its lyrics.

Ms. Mockingbird

She sits high in the catbird seat, repeats
each neighbor's favorite song:
towhee's trill and swallow's twitter,
crow's caw-cah and sparrow's chitter,
more than thirty, each one new.
She can go an hour or two, fool you
into looking for a robin red as dawn
or a finch that flits its yellow shape
across warm summer morns.
Perhaps you'll be surprised to find,
high in the old gray sycamore,
a bird whose beauty isn't strained
in vain attempt to make display
audacious as a cardinal or saucy as a jay.
In fact she's gray. But oh, her song!
I would not trade it for
a blue-faced,
green-eyed,
red-legged,
yellow-spotted,
ruby-throated,
puce-booted
booby.

Teacher, help me, pleeze!

Why bother with e's in bee or be?
How come there is no c in sea or see, no I in
dye or eye, no 2 in two or too or to?
The o in owe is much too strong, it overpowers
you and me (we); the a in aye does that to you (ye).
H is just a breath away, disappears in Oh—O ware
does it go? Please tell me wen to stop. Eye can't
control myself at awl, and I'm afraid I'll p.
Why are so many vowels left in queue? Why are
they made to stand in line? Since they have to wait
I think they should be given scones and t.
U'd do at least that much for me.
While we're on u, can u explain the double u in we?
And what's the use of double u in ewe?
Is ex an x that went away, and if so Y?
And r u tired of this bi now?
You need to get some z's, pleeze.

How a Lepidoptera Survived A Rapid Rapids Ride

A curled leaf slips around and down
a frothy churn of spume. On it,
riding each surprise, a caterpillar
clutches cilia which each leaf hides.
It's just so basic, but who believes
there's beauty in a worm? A cat,
perhaps, would make us try to
rescue it from drowning, but we
just don't believe a caterpillar can.

When it lands it can turn into moth
or butterfly, the former heir to wooly
things, the latter made to beautify.
Choices sometimes hide in dreams
or signals from anticipating minds.
Let's keep the cat now that it's had
its ride and look at caterpillars that
surprise by what's inside: cat is
caterpillar's multilingual guide.

In Italian, French and Latin, German,
Dutch, and even otherwise the folk
who lived by rivers where our languages
survived say the cat in caterpillar has
a history as hairy as it's wise. We may
think the color yellow was derived
by what you can perceive with eyes.
Look it up in early Dutch* and I think
you'll be surprised.

---
*boterschijte

About the Author

Curt Curtin has won poetry awards including the *Jacob Knight Award* (2005), the Worcester County Poetry Association's *Frank O'Hara Award* (2010), and the Connecticut Poetry Society's annual contest (2019). He has twice been named a Pushcart Prize nominee. His poetry has been published in a variety of journals and anthologies. Many of the poems in this collection have been classroom-tested in two schools.

Curt has been a volunteer poetry teacher in a fifth grade Magnet School program funded by a state grant. He taught English and Creative Writing at the junior high, high school and college levels for over 25 years. He has also served as a Court Appointed Special Advocate (CASA) for children in foster care and was a Volunteer Case Reviewer for the Massachusetts Department of Children and Families for over 20 years.

www.ingramcontent.com/pod-product-compliance
Lightning Source LLC
Chambersburg PA
CBHW060226050426
42446CB00013B/3189